Piano Solo

THE WORLD'S GREAT CLASSICAL MUSIC

Mozart

45 Selections from Symphonies, Concertos, Operas, Ballets and Piano Works

Intermediate to Advanced Piano Solos

EDITED BY BLAKE NEELY AND RICHARD WALTERS

Cover Painting: Goya, *The Meadow*, 1788

ISBN 0-634-01636-9

7777 W. BLUEMOUND RD. P.O. BOX 13819 MILWAUKEE, WI 53213

Visit Hal Leonard Online at
www.halleonard.com

CONTENTS

Pieces originally for solo piano; the remaining works are transcriptions.

Wolfgang Amadeus Mozart
January 27, 1756—December 5, 1791

The short life of Wolfgang Amadeus Mozart was one of extremes. As a child he was the toast of the courts of Europe. Yet as an adult he found those same courts unwilling to offer him permanent employment. While his strikingly accomplished childhood compositions amused and amazed the public, many of the operas he wrote as an adult were too musically and dramatically sophisticated for the public of his own Vienna. Much of his music was only fully appreciated after his death. Mozart would come to be revered as one of the world's greatest musical geniuses, creating symphonies, operas, ballets, masses, sonatas, concertos, marches, songs and pieces for both vocal and instrumental ensembles, much of which is still in the repertoire today. Although he earned comparatively large amounts of money for his time, he faced continual financial problems. By breaking away from the established system of musicians working within the courts of nobility and church leaders, he created the now legendary figure of the struggling artist.

Wolfgang and his older sister Nannerl were remarkable musical prodigies, born into a cultural climate of fascination with prodigies. Their father Leopold Mozart, a court musician in Salzburg who was best known for a treatise on the violin, launched his children on a lengthy concert tour when Wolfgang was just six. At the tour's end, by which time the boy was nearly eleven, he had seen and experienced more than most people of his era could hope for in a lifetime. Young Wolfgang was so charming and precocious that after playing for Austrian Empress Maria Theresa, he climbed up on her lap, threw his arms around her neck and kissed her. Remarkably, she allowed this breach of protocol.

The charm of a child prodigy fades as the child grows, and so did Mozart's popularity. Public concerts were just coming into fashion during his childhood, which allowed Leopold to market his children's talents to the general public as well as to the elite minority. But both audiences viewed the children as something of a circus act: They were more interested in their ability to play the keyboard with a cloth laid over the keys than in their ability to sight read and improvise at great length.

Returning to his Salzburg home, the young Wolfgang received numerous commissions. In 1767 Leopold took the children to Vienna in hopes of a similar reception. But those hopes were dashed when a smallpox epidemic struck the city, infecting both Wolfgang and Nannerl. Although both recovered, Wolfgang was now 12. He had outgrown prodigy status, but was still too young to compete with such veterans of Viennese musical life as the Haydn brothers, Franz Joseph and Michael, and Christoph Willibald Gluck.

Father and son traveled to Italy in 1769, leaving Nannerl and her mother in Salzburg. Nannerl gave music lessons to support the family and pay for her brother's travels. Mozart charmed Italian audiences, singing and playing the harpsichord and violin, and displaying his astonishing ability to write out an entire piece after having heard it just once. Here the young composer received several promising commissions and first displayed his remarkable ability to write Italian opera. But the fickle nature of court politics found Wolfgang back in Salzburg by 1773, trying to resign himself to life as a court musician. But provincial Salzburg, and the role of servant to the archbishop, was too stifling for a brilliant seventeen-year-old who had been applauded throughout Europe.

Wolfgang continued to compose despite his frustration, producing the stunning *Exsultate Jubilate* and several symphonies. A commission came from the court at Munich for an opera buffa, raising the family's hopes once again. Wolfgang spent over a year in Munich, where he was treated with deference and saw successful performances of a number of his works. After this heady experience he returned to the dreary confines of his post in Salzburg, playing the violin and composing as required by the archbishop.

In August of 1777, at the age of twenty-one, Wolfgang reached the end of his tether in Salzburg and resigned his position as a musician in the court of the archbishop. Soon afterward, he and his mother, Anna Maria Mozart, left on what would prove a fateful trip. The pair arrived in Munich where Mozart's dissatisfaction with his previous post, and his less than cordial departure from the Salzburg court, had become known. No one in Munich would hire him, nor in Augsburg. Wolfgang moved on to Mannheim, where he could not secure a post but did find inspiration in the city's rich musical climate. He also fell in love with a singer named Aloysia Weber. He pressed on to Paris in hopes of finding work and acclaim there.

In Paris mother and son found themselves in financial straits. Wolfgang had written to his father in February: "I will gladly give lessons as a favor, especially when I see that my pupil has talent, inclination, and a desire to learn; but to be forced to go to a house at a particular hour, or to have to wait at home for a pupil—that is something that I cannot do, no matter how much money I might earn." By March he was taking pupils. The only post offered to him in Paris was an uninteresting one at the palace of Versailles. In June, in the midst of this disappointment, his mother's health began to deteriorate. She died on July 3, leaving Wolfgang alone, isolated and grief stricken. Out of concern for his father he wrote home just saying that his mother was ill. To a family friend he wrote a letter containing the truth, asking him to prepare his father for the news which he would send home in a few days.

Wolfgang returned to Salzburg, at his father's urging, to rejoin the court of the archbishop as organist and composer. He wrote several pieces at this time for a traveling theater company, including a *singspiel*, or German opera that mixed dialog and song, entitled *Zaïde*. Life in the court was becoming intolerable and Wolfgang's relationship with the archbishop was sliding into blatant hostility. Wolfgang was fired while in Vienna, in service of the court. He wrote to his father of the dismissal: "Now please be cheerful, for my happiness is just beginning." He told his father that he wanted nothing more to do with Salzburg. Leopold tried to repair the damage, but the result was a now famous meeting between Wolfgang and the archbishop's chief steward. The steward gave Wolfgang a dressing down for his defiance and then used his foot to expel him from the room. Mozart's Salzburg days were officially and decisively over.

An impoverished Wolfgang took up residence in the Weber family house, where his former love Aloysia lived, though she had long since rejected him. A commission to write *The Abduction from the Seraglio* brightened his prospects. In December of 1781 he wrote to his father that he had become engaged to Aloysia's sister Constanze, saying, "She is not witty, but she has enough sound common sense to be able to fulfill her duties as wife and mother." Although the overbearing Leopold never fully approved of the marriage, the couple was wed in 1782. They would have six children, only two of whom would survive to adulthood.

Though continually plagued by financial problems Wolfgang had great musical successes in Vienna, writing such pieces as the Piano Concertos Nos. 20, 21 and 22. He also wrote some of his great symphonies at this time, including No. 35 ("Haffner") and No. 36 ("Linz"). During 1785, the revered Franz Joseph Haydn wrote to Leopold saying, "Your son is the greatest composer I know, either in person or by reputation..."

In 1786 his opera *The Marriage of Figaro* got a mixed reaction in Vienna. The next year Wolfgang had tremendous success conducting *Figaro* in Prague, which resulted in another commission. On the heels of that success came the sad news that his father had died. Leopold had been his son's most ardent supporter, life-long confidant and advisor, although in later years Wolfgang had chosen to ignore much of that advice. In August, still grieving the loss of his father, Mozart created one of his best-loved works, the serenade *Eine kleine Nacht Musik* for string quartet plus double bass. In October he rushed to complete the opera *Don Giovanni*, in fulfillment of the Prague commission. Legend has it that he did not write the overture until two days before the premiere.

By 1788, Wolfgang was in financial difficulties. *Don Giovanni*, which had been a huge success in Prague, was a failure in Vienna. In June of that year his daughter died. In July he completed two of his greatest symphonies, the tragic Symphony No. 40, followed in August by the stunning Symphony No. 41 ("Jupiter"). In January of 1790, Wolfgang's opera *Così fan tutte* was premiered in Vienna, to audiences that failed to understand the subtleties of the plot. Despite the fact that Mozart's rival Antonio Salieri is believed to have plotted to delay the opera's premiere, there is absolutely no evidence to support the legend that he was in any way responsible for Mozart's untimely death.

Through these difficulties, Wolfgang's health began to suffer, exacerbated by his life-long frustration over never winning the royal appointment he felt he deserved. Despite his increasingly fragile health and personal stress he maintained his exceptional musical productivity. In 1791, an unsigned letter from an anonymous source offered a commission for a requiem. Long the subject of much speculation, the letter is believed to have come from Count Franz von Walsegg who wanted to buy the piece and take credit for its composition in honor of his dead wife. Walsegg's servant delivered the letter.

Wolfgang worked at a feverish pace, completing the opera *La Clemenza di Tito* in 18 days. He also completed *The Magic Flute* in time for a September 30 premiere. It would be his last opera. He worked to complete the *Requiem*, stopping a few bars into the "Lacrymosa" movement. The piece was completed later by his pupil, Süssmayer. In the early hours of December 5, in Vienna, Mozart died of rheumatic inflammatory fever. Legends, many of which persist to this day, began to appear almost immediately following the announcement of his death.

Mozart would come to be hailed as the greatest composer of his era, perhaps of any era, with his symphonies, operas, concertos and chamber music recognized as staples of the standard repertoire. Salzburg, the town Mozart was so anxious to put behind him, has created an industry out of the composer's life and work. Mozart's place in history is unaffected by his pauper's funeral, attended by just a few close friends, and burial in a common grave. What better testament to the composer's rare talent and enduring genius than the words of Albert Einstein: "Mozart is the greatest composer of all. Beethoven 'created' his music, but the music of Mozart is of such purity and beauty that one feels he merely 'found' it—that it has always existed as part of the inner beauty of the universe waiting to be revealed."

—Elaine Schmidt

Ave verum corpus

Wolfgang Amadeus Mozart
1756–1791
K 618
originally for chorus and orchestra

Turkish Finale
from the opera THE ABDUCTION FROM THE SERAGLIO

Wolfgang Amadeus Mozart
1756-1791
originally for orchestra

Allegro Vivace

Vedrai, carino
from the opera DON GIOVANNI

Wolfgang Amadeus Mozart
1756–1791

14

Là ci darem la mano
from the opera DON GIOVANNI

Wolfgang Amadeus Mozart
1756–1791

18

Minuet
from the opera DON GIOVANNI

Wolfgang Amadeus Mozart
1756–1791

Moderato

Eine kleine Nachtmusik

(A Little Night Music)
First Movement Excerpt

Wolfgang Amadeus Mozart
1756-1791
K 525
originally for string ensemble

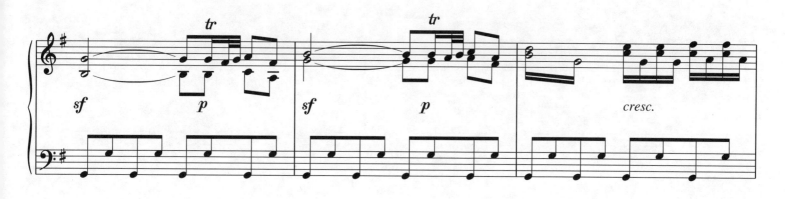

Eine kleine Nachtmusik

(A Little Night Music)

Second Movement Excerpt, "Romanza"

Wolfgang Amadeus Mozart
1756-1791
K 525
originally for string ensemble

Eine kleine Nachtmusik
(A Little Night Music)
Fourth Movement Excerpt, "Rondo"

Wolfgang Amadeus Mozart
1756-1791
K 525
originally for string ensemble

Horn Concerto No. 3 in E-flat Major
Third Movement Excerpt

Wolfgang Amadeus Mozart
1756-1791
K 447
originally for French horn and orchestra

Allegro

Alleluia
from the solo motet EXSULTATE, JUBILATE
Excerpt

Wolfgang Amadeus Mozart
1756–1791
K 165
originally for soprano and orchestra

Allegro non troppo

43

Fantasia in D Minor

Wolfgang Amadeus Mozart
1756–1791
K 397

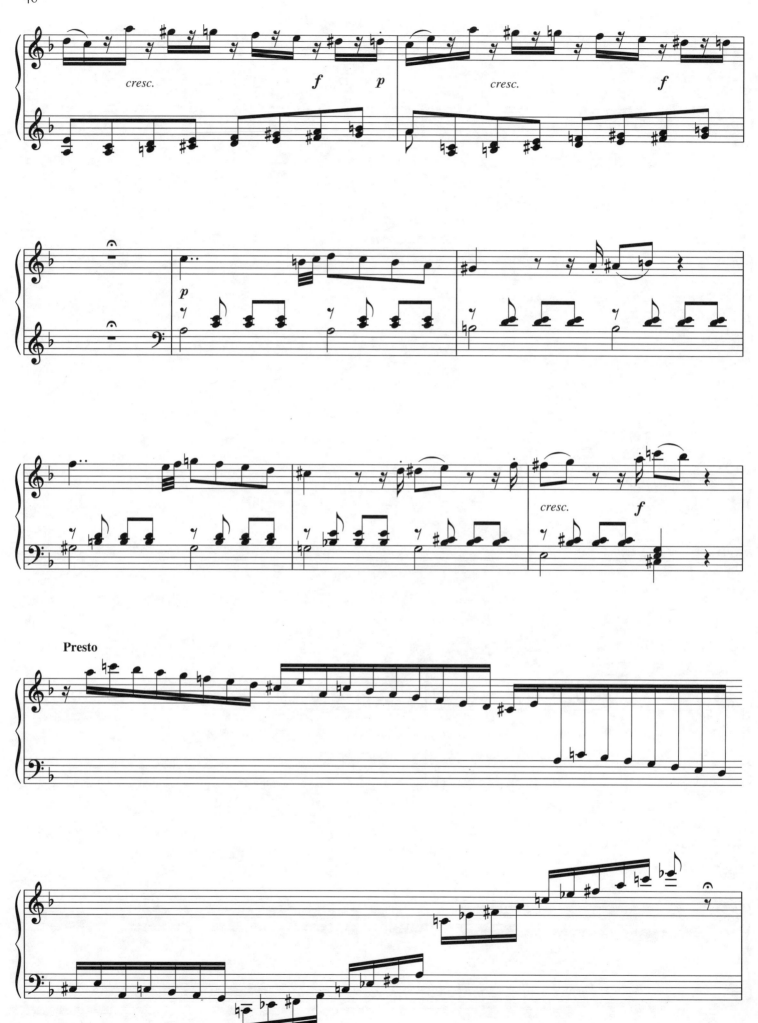

Tempo primo

Allegretto

Ach, ich fühl's
from the opera DIE ZAUBERFLÖTE
(The Magic Flute)

Wolfgang Amadeus Mozart
1756–1791

Andante

Papageno's Song
from the opera THE MAGIC FLUTE

Wolfgang Amadeus Mozart
1756–1791

Dies Bildnis ist bezaubernd schön
from the opera DIE ZAUBERFLÖTE
(The Magic Flute)

Wolfgang Amadeus Mozart
1756–1791

Queen of the Night's Vengeance Aria

from the opera THE MAGIC FLUTE

Wolfgang Amadeus Mozart
1756–1791
originally for soprano and orchestra

Allegro assai

Deh vieni, non tardar
from the opera LE NOZZE DI FIGARO
(The Marriage of Figaro)

Wolfgang Amadeus Mozart
1756–1791

March
from the opera LE NOZZE DI FIGARO
(The Marriage of Figaro)

Wolfgang Amadeus Mozart
1756-1791
originally for orchestra and chorus

69

Porgi, amor

from the opera LE NOZZE DI FIGARO
(The Marriage of Figaro)

Wolfgang Amadeus Mozart
1756–1791

Larghetto

Voi, che sapete

from the opera LE NOZZE DI FIGARO
(The Marriage of Figaro)

Wolfgang Amadeus Mozart
1756–1791

Andante con moto

Piano Concerto No. 21 in C Major

"Elvira Madigan"
Second Movement Excerpt

Wolfgang Amadeus Mozart
1756–1791
K 467
originally for piano and orchestra

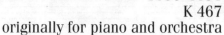

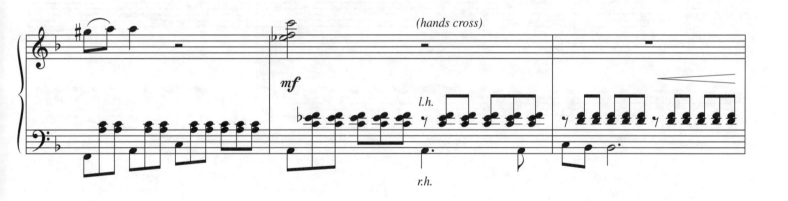

Agnus Dei
from MASS IN C ("Coronation")
Excerpt

Wolfgang Amadeus Mozart
1756-1791
K 317
originally for soprano and orchestra

82

Piano Concerto No. 20 in D Minor
Second Movement Excerpt, "Romanza"

Wolfgang Amadeus Mozart
1756-1791
K 466
originally for piano and orchestra

Andante cantabile

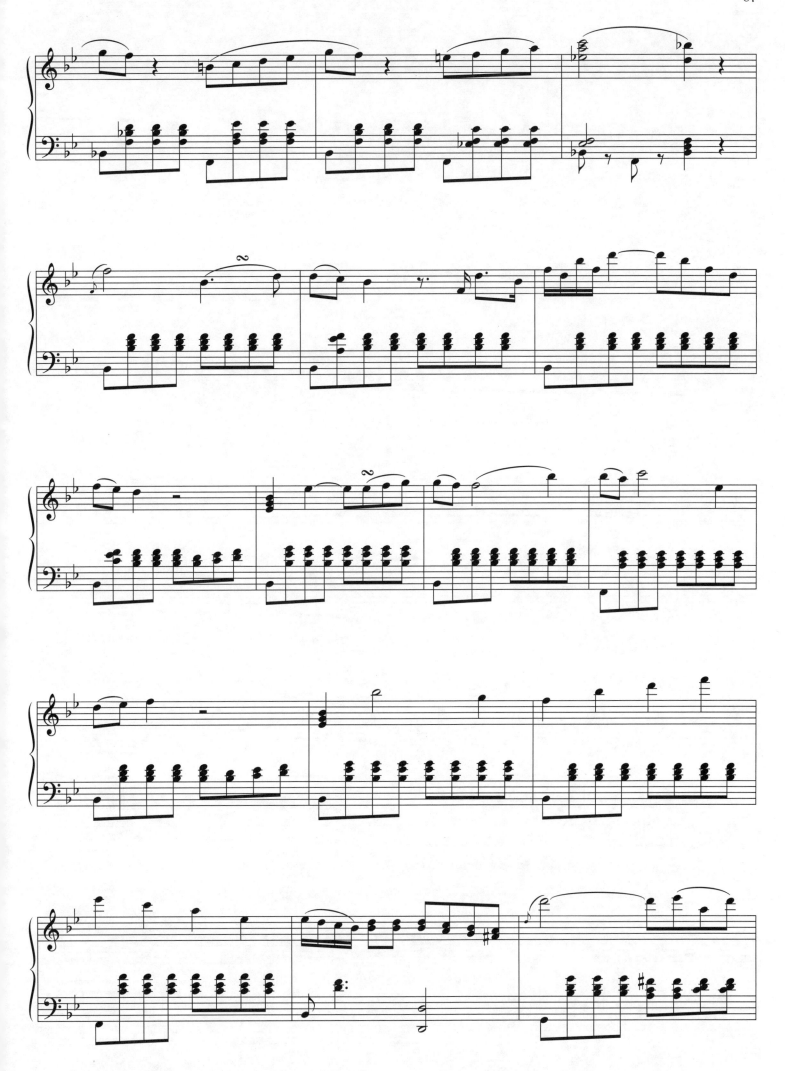

Piano Concerto No. 27 in B-flat Major
Third Movement Excerpt

Wolfgang Amadeus Mozart
1756-1791
K 595
originally for piano and orchestra

Piano Concerto No. 22 in E-flat Major
Third Movement Excerpt

Wolfgang Amadeus Mozart
1756-1791
K 482
originally for piano and orchestra

Lacrymosa

from REQUIEM

Wolfgang Amadeus Mozart
1756–1791
K 626
originally for chorus and orchestra

Larghetto

Dies irae
from REQUIEM

Wolfgang Amadeus Mozart
1756-1791
K 626
originally for chorus and orchestra

Allegro assai

105

Rondo in D Major

Wolfgang Amadeus Mozart
1756–1791
K 485

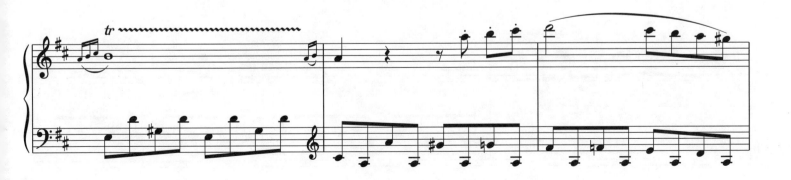

112

Serenade No. 10 for Winds
Third Movement

Wolfgang Amadeus Mozart
1756-1791
K 361
originally for woodwinds

Sinfonie Concertante
First Movement Themes

Wolfgang Amadeus Mozart
1756-1791
K 364
originally for orchestra, violin and viola

Sonata in A Major

Third Movement
"Rondo alla Turca"

Wolfgang Amadeus Mozart
1756–1791
K 331

Alla Turca

Allegretto

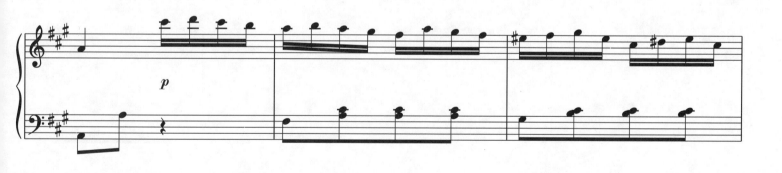

Sonata in C Major

Wolfgang Amadeus Mozart
1756–1791
K 545

Andante

142

146

Rondo
[Allegretto]

[mf]

Sonata in A Minor
First Movement

Wolfgang Amadeus Mozart
1756–1791
K 310

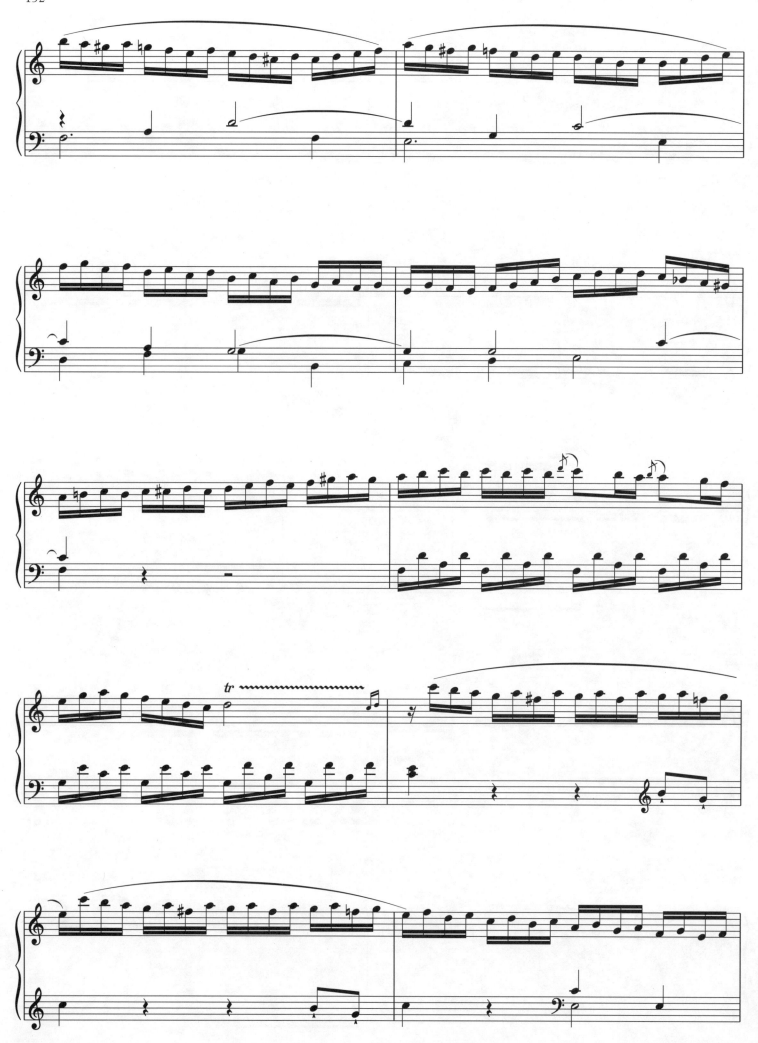

156

Sonatina No. 6 in C Major

Third Movement
"Finale"

Wolfgang Amadeus Mozart
1756–1791

Symphony No. 25 in G Minor
First Movement Excerpt

Wolfgang Amadeus Mozart
1756-1791
K 183
originally for orchestra

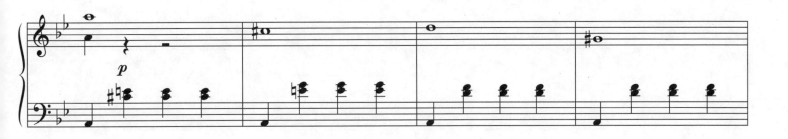

172

Symphony No. 38 in D Major
"Prague"
First Movement Excerpt

Wolfgang Amadeus Mozart
1756–1791
K 504
originally for orchestra

174

Symphony No. 29 in A Major
First Movement Excerpt

Wolfgang Amadeus Mozart
1756–1791
K 201
originally for orchestra

Allegro moderato

Symphony No. 35 in D Major

"Haffner"
First Movement Excerpt

Wolfgang Amadeus Mozart
1756–1791
K 385
originally for orchestra

Symphony No. 36 in C Major
"Linz"
First Movement Excerpt

Wolfgang Amadeus Mozart
1756-1791
K 425
originally for orchestra

Allegro

Symphony No. 40 in G Minor

First Movement Excerpt

Wolfgang Amadeus Mozart
1756–1791
K 550
originally for orchestra

Symphony No. 40 in G Minor
Third Movement, "Minuet"

Wolfgang Amadeus Mozart
1756-1791
K 550
originally for orchestra

L'istesso tempo

Symphony No. 41 in C Major
"Jupiter"
First Movement Excerpt

Wolfgang Amadeus Mozart
1756–1791
K 551
originally for orchestra

Allegro vivace

Symphony No. 41 in C Major
"Jupiter"
Third Movement Excerpt, "Minuet"

Wolfgang Amadeus Mozart
1756-1791
K 551
originally for orchestra

Variations on
"Ah, vous dirais-je, maman"

(Twinkle, Twinkle, Little Star)

Wolfgang Amadeus Mozart
1756–1791
K 265

Theme

Allegretto

1st- *mf*
2nd- *pp*

Var. I

mp

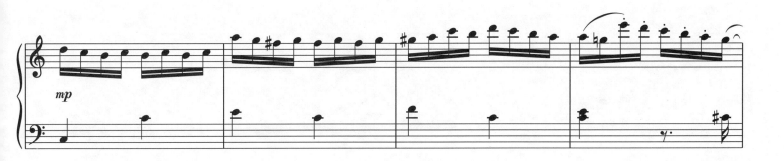

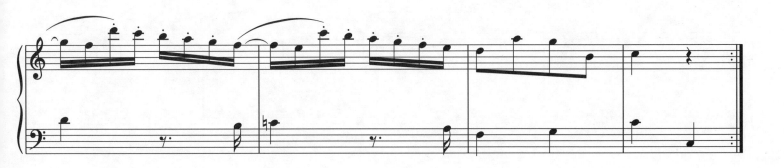

Var. II

Var. III

212

Var. IV

Var. V

Var. VI

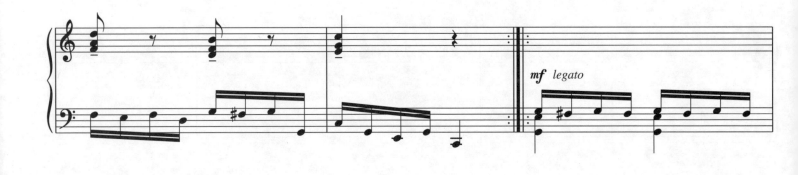

Var. VII

Laudate Dominum
from VESPERAE SOLENNES DE CONFESSORE

Wolfgang Amadeus Mozart
1756-1791
K 339
originally for soprano, orchestra and chorus

Andante ma un poco sostenuto

221

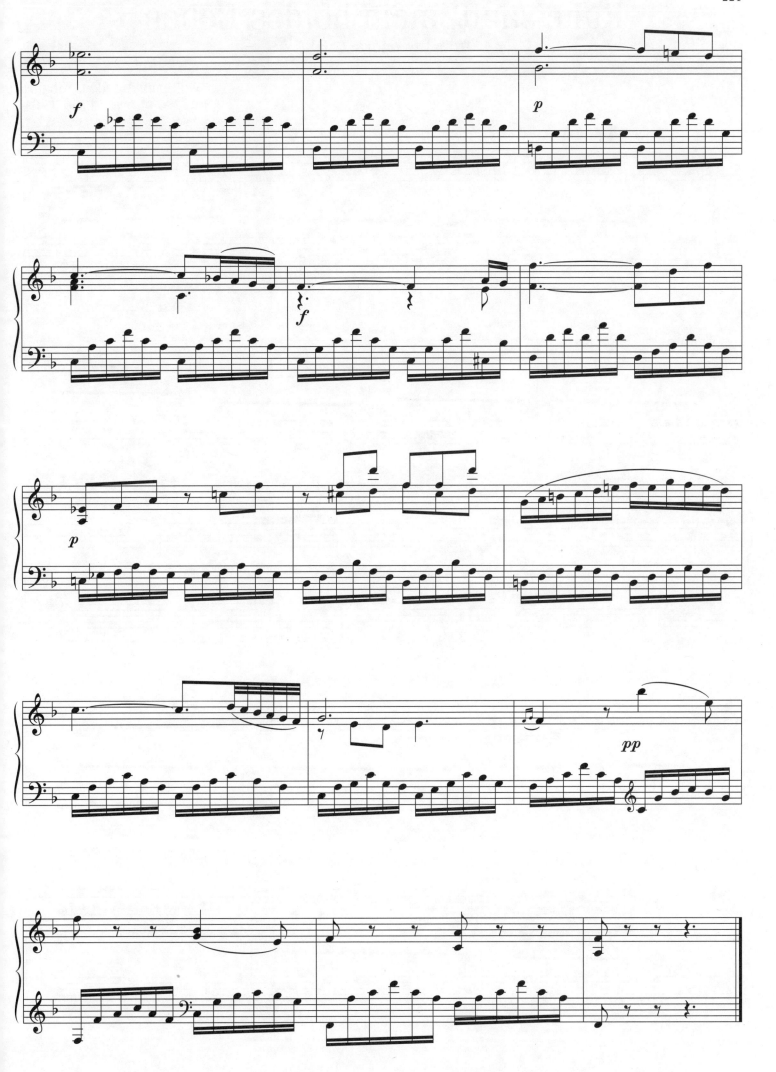

Ruhe sanft, mein holdes Leben
from the opera ZAÏDE

Wolfgang Amadeus Mozart
1756-1791

Tempo di Menuetto grazioso